Ex-Voto

Tupelo Press Poetry in Translation

Abiding Places: Korea, South and North, by Ko Un
Translated from Korean by Hillel Schwartz and Sunny Jung

Invitation to a Secret Feast: Selected Poems, by Joumana Haddad
Translated from Arabic by Khaled Mattawa with Najib Awad, Issa Boullata,
Marilyn Hacker, Joumana Haddad, Henry Matthews, and David Harsent

Night, Fish and Charlie Parker, by Phan Nhien Hao
Translated from Vietnamese by Linh Dinh

Stone Lyre: Poems of René Char
Translated from French by Nancy Naomi Carlson

This Lamentable City: Poems of Polina Barskova
Translated from Russian by Ilya Kaminsky with Katie Farris, Rachel Galvin, and
Matthew Zapruder

New Cathay: Contemporary Chinese Poetry
Edited by Ming Di and translated from Chinese by Nick Admussen, Neil Aitken,
Tony Barnstone, Ming Di, Katie Farris, Eleanor Goodman, Kerry Shawn Keys,
Jennifer Kronovet, Dian Li, Christopher Lupke, Cody Reese, Elizabeth Reitzell,
Jonathan Stalling, Ao Wang, and Afaa M. Weaver

Ex-Voto, by Adélia Prado
Translated from Brazilian Portugese by Ellen Doré Watson

Ex-Voto

Poems

Adélia Prado

*Translated from Brazilian Portuguese
by Ellen Doré Watson*

Tupelo Press
North Adams, Massachusetts

Library of Congress Cataloging-in-Publication Data
Prado, Adélia.
[Poems. Selections]
Ex-Voto : poems / Adélia Prado ; translated from Brazilian Portuguese by Ellen Dore
Watson. — First edition.
    pages cm. — (Tupelo Press Poetry in Translation)
ISBN 978-1-936797-30-1 (pbk. original : alk. paper)
I. Watson, Ellen, 1950– translator. II. Title.
PQ9698.26.R29E9 2013
869.1'42—dc23   2013014998

First edition: June 2013.

Cover and text designed by Katherine Kimball.
Cover photograph: Jeffrey Levine, "Archetype I," 2013. Used by courtesy of the artist.

Tupelo Press
P.O. Box 1767, 243 Union Street, Eclipse Mill, Loft 305
North Adams, Massachusetts 01247
Telephone: (413) 664–9611 / Fax: (413) 664–9711
editor@tupelopress.org / www.tupelopress.org

Tupelo Press is an award-winning independent literary press that publishes fine fiction,
nonfiction, and poetry in books that are a joy to hold as well as read. Tupelo Press is
a registered 501(c)3 nonprofit organization, and we rely on public support to carry out
our mission of publishing extraordinary work that may be outside the realm of large
commercial publishers. Financial donations are welcome and are tax deductible.

Published with support of the National Endowment for the Arts and the Brazilian Ministry
of Culture / Foundation of the National Library (*Obra publicada com o apoio do Ministério da
Cultura do Brasil / Fundação Biblioteca Nacional*).

ART WORKS.
arts.gov

MINISTÉRIO DA CULTURA
Fundação BIBLIOTECA NACIONAL

The poems in *Ex-Voto* are drawn from:

O Pelicano (The Pelican), 1987

A Faca no Peito (Knife in the Chest), 1988

Oráculos do Maio (Oracles of May), 1999

Books of Adélia Prado's poetry previously published in English, translated by Ellen Doré Watson:

The Alphabet in the Park: Selected Poems of Adélia Prado

(Wesleyan University Press, 1990)

The Headlong Heart

(chapbook, Livingston University Press, 1988)

Contents

Foreword

Ilya Kaminsky

"It's the Soul That's Erotic"

Reading the poetry of Adélia Prado, like reading the work of any true mystic, you may find yourself standing in front of the proverbial brick wall of Sir Edward B. Taylor's often-quoted definition of prayer: "the address of personal spirit to personal spirit."

If prayer is so personal, what are the means by which this can become a work of art? How can anyone put an address like that into language without sounding artificial? And in our time, what does it mean to be a mystic?

The term *mystic* may mislead or intimidate—the prestige accorded to the word has traditionally been so exalted, and some people feel that such heightened perception and joy must be attainable only by a few human beings. This is far from the case. Mystical experience is always available, and to anyone.

How so? A poem by Fernando Pessoa, another poet of the Portuguese language, may be of use to us here:

> If they want me to be a mystic, fine. I'm a mystic.
> I'm a mystic, but only of the body.
> My soul is simple and doesn't think.
>
> My mysticism is not wanting to know.
> It's living without thinking about it.
>
> I don't know what Nature is. I sing it.
> I live on a hilltop
> In a solitary whitewashed cabin.
> And that's what it is all about.[1]

Is Adélia Prado a mystic? A devout Catholic, she announces, "I am a woman with whom God toys." She speaks of God, yet her poems are full of sexuality, of senses, of guts. The best person to describe her poetics would be not the Pope in Rome but Romanian philosopher Emil Cioran:

> Think of God and not of religion, of ecstasy and not spirituality. The difference between the theoretician of faith and the believer is as great as between the psychiatrist and the psychotic.[2]

According to her longtime translator Ellen Doré Watson, Prado "prays daily, in solitude and also regularly with one or two other local women, an intimate ritualistic reciting of prayers they all know by heart." And then she writes.

She addresses her prayers because "A voluptuous woman in her bed / can praise God, / even if she is nothing but voluptuous and happy."[3] Her addresses are fierce, frank, outrageous, and sensual:

> What I have to tell you
> Is of such high order and so precious
> That if I kept it to myself
> It would feel like stealing:
> The asshole is beautiful!
> ("Object of Affection")

The eroticism on every page in these poems expresses utter devotion. According to Watson, the work is "oral in nature, and comprises an ongoing spiritual journey, but—despite her alternating resistance and acceptance of her role as God's mouthpiece—Prado's is not a collective or imparting voice, but a searching, struggling, interior one." The humor in her poems is laughing at the edge of the abyss: she has spent years in darkest depression. The tension between these two states produces poetry.

> With me it's wild parties
> or strict piety.

I didn't deserve to be born,
to eat with a mouth, walk on two feet
and carry inside me twenty-five feet of guts
("The Third Way")

*

Born in Minas Gerais, the second most populous of Brazil's twenty-six states, Adélia Prado has spent all her life in that landlocked place of rugged mountains, mines, and baroque churches. "Of my entire family I am the only one who has seen the ocean," she says.[4]

What was her family like? They were laborers, whose men worked the railroad and whose women, including her mother and grandmother, died in childbirth.

Although she started writing when very young, Prado, herself the mother of five grown children, showed no one her work and began to consider it poetry only in her late thirties, when she completed the manuscript of her first collection.

Before that, she taught in public schools for twenty-five years.

Prado's literary career began late—and with a bang—when the elder statesman of Brazilian poetry, Carlos Drummond de Andrade (1902–1987), announced in his Rio de Janeiro newspaper column that Saint Francis was dictating verses to a housewife in Minas Gerais.

Her book-release party was an important cultural event, where such luminaries as Clarice Lispector and Drummond de Andrade hailed and welcomed the poet.

*

So, what was Saint Francis dictating to her? Let's see what Prado has to say:

Interviewer: Can you tell us—what is God?

Adélia Prado: No, no, I don't know! Good heavens, no! What is God?
No . . . We tend to be attracted to the un-nameable, the ineffable.
I think art reaches towards this as well. Despite the artists who

claim to be atheists. Drummond has a poem . . .

Interviewer: Drummond said he was an atheist.

Prado: No, Drummond was not really an atheist. He thought that would be going too far. He spoke agnostic. There's a poem in which he practically apologizes just for wanting to believe. Really. It's wonderful! The transcendent is made manifest in spite of the poet himself. That's poetry's revenge: it's bigger than we are.

You have only twenty-four hours a day. No one has more than that. And in this tiny, impoverished, limited bit of experience, I'm to find an explanation for the absurdity of my existence and the world. Metaphysics resides in the daily. Ortega y Gasset said: "It's the philosopher's gift to admire what is natural." It's the gift of the poet!

It is our craft. It gives us pleasure, not pain. What hurts is life.[5]

★

Here is why I find this poet refreshing:

In antiquity, poets were revered as figures of divine proximity: in the public's imagination, they stood somewhere between soothsayers and demigods. Indeed, deities themselves were often the audience for poets, as in the myth of Orpheus.

When people call someone a poet these days, they often mean to imply that she or he is "romantic," at best—or a scoundrel at worst. The Romantic idea of a poet as a Don Juan was the creation of the nineteenth century, and the view of a poet as a rascal corresponded to popular portrayals of such "outlaw" poets as Villon, Marlow, Mayakovsky. Today in the West, poets have mostly become either low-level entertainers or academics (the problem is not that poets are professors or stand-up comics, but that they *write* like professors or stand-up comics).

Prado does not fit any of these templates. She writes out of the very elements. In her world, if a poet is a professor, she is a professor of the five senses, as Garcia Lorca suggested a poet must be.

Ellen Doré Watson interviewed Prado for *BOMB* magazine:

EDW: On a personal level, then, not in terms of the church, do you ever feel that your faith is fighting your poetry?

Prado: No, and that's good you ask me that, because I found God more deeply in poetry than in doctrine. I realized that the poetic experience is in fact deeply sacred and religious.

EDW: What about the reader who has no faith?

Prado: Well, the reader who doesn't care about religion will consider the religious content to be only poetic. He'll say, "You are talking about God, but I don't care about God, I care about poetry." That's okay; you do what you want. But it's not like that for me: The poetic experience is sacred.[6]

★

American poets as a rule tend to mistrust her kind of voice, and yet Prado has found a devoted following. How so? Perhaps this is because her addresses to her God never take a conventional route:

> When I clamor for God, He sends me back to time,
> to receipts which
> —by order of the government—
> I must demand of shady shopkeepers.
> Why all this weight on my shoulders?
> I didn't ask to be the inspector of the world,
> I want to sin, to be free,
> leave the thieves
> to their tax obligations.
>> ("The Good Shepherd")

Prado's loftiness of address works because she constantly doubts that voice, struggles with it, plays with it, sexes it. She refuses the professional labels:

> I don't like to think of myself as a *writer.* I hate the idea of being an established author who gives advice to other people. I want to be a new author. I want to feel—with any book I come to write—the

same doubt, the same anxiety, the same joy I felt when I wrote my first poems. I always want to be in that precarious, difficult position. Writing is artificial: "making literature." Writing is not a natural condition. I think it was Joyce's *Ulysses* that opened my eyes to free association, to the way the mind works: I say *banana* and I think *potato;* I say *cup* and I think *eyeglasses.*[7]

Is Prado naïve? Childish? Here is Milosz, another poet who warned against the bureaucratization of literature in our time:

In the twentieth century, as never before, poets were forced to resist pressure of facts that run contrary to their somewhat childish natures . . . Simone Weil was courageous. If she considered something true, she would say it, without fear of being labeled . . . The poet of today, enmeshed in various professional rituals, is too ashamed to attain such frankness. Of what is he ashamed? Of the child in himself who wants the earth to be flat.[8]

An instructive moment for a North American reader comes when Prado dismisses the mode that is so pervasive in our poetry:

I don't want to tell stories;
stories are the excrement of time.
　　("The Sphinx")

★

I mention Milosz and think of Whitman, the poet Milosz claimed to follow. Of course, the children of Whitman in other countries are many—Mayakovsky of Russia, Anna Swir of Poland, Apollinaire of France, Yonna Wollach of Israel, Tomaš Šalamun of Slovenia. Allen Ginsberg, who dreamed of Whitman in supermarkets, said a cockroach is holy. Prado says an asshole is beautiful. Her lists of "old people [who] spit with absolutely no finesse / and bicycles [that] bully traffic on the sidewalk" make me think of Whitman also.

Just as one may tire of Whitman's American gigantism, at times one might also tire of Prado's God, and yet in both poets it is the sensual world (captured in changes of tone and textures of language) that propels us to go on. Whitman brings erotica into his very syntax, alliteration, assonance, when we least expect; Prado uses tonal shifts—she tells Saint Anthony to go find her wallet. And we are rewarded with streets "where virgins stroll. Like heads of garlic . . ." ("Lily-Like"), and with the fierceness of a voice that says:

> I love, love you, love you,
> sad as you are, O world . . .
>> ("Fibrillations")

★

What is her God? Prado's *Ismália says: "God is a brick, right here on my dog's nose."* ("The Third Way") Then Prado says what Whitman might have said:

> I don't have the nerve
> to approach God up close like Ismália,
> that's why I just yelp,
> and approach men up close.
> I smell Pedro's shirt,
> Jonathan's bitter aftertaste.

But Prado is also *not* Whitman, as she admits that in her poems Jonathan is a name for Jesus:

> I love Jonathan.
> There you have it: the monotonous, diarrheal subject.
> "He wants to see you," said a voice in a dream.
> And thus were unleashed the forms in which God hides.
> You could worship tufts of grass, sand,
> and not discover where oboes come from.
> Jonathan wants to see me,
> so he will.

The Devil howls, handcuffed down in hell,
while I
tear my body from my clothes.
          ("The Battle")

                          ★

So how should a twenty-first-century poet and mystic talk about her
God?

Well, how do others speak about God?

For the theologian Paul Tillich, a personal god was an absurdity,
"a being among beings" rather than Being.

For Martin Heidegger, God was the Nothing that gives rise to
existence.

For Martin Buber, God was personal but was discovered in con-
tact with other people. Life itself, then, was an interrelationship with
God.

Julian of Norwich spoke of Christ the mother.

"Jesus, are you not my mother?" asked Margueritte d'Oignt.

Ramakrishna spoke of God as mother and of revelation as a
white fish she cooks.

And Yehuda Amichai tells us, "God's hand is in the world like my
mother's hand is in the guts of the slaughtered chicken."[9]

Here is Prado:

God is better-looking than I am.
And He's not young.
That's consolation.
          ("Parameter")

And again, here's Prado:

We give birth to life between our legs
and go on talking about it till the end,
few of us understanding:
it's the soul that's erotic.

If I want, I put on a Bach aria
so I can feel forgiving and calm.
What I understand of God is His wrath;
there's no other way to say it.
The ball thumping against the wall annoys me,
but the kids laugh, contented.
I've seen hundreds of afternoons like today.
No agony, just an anxious impatience:
something is going to happen.
Destiny doesn't exist.
It's God we need, and fast.[10]

*

We need God, and fast, this poet says—but what of those of us who don't feel such need?

The place of religion in the modern world has clearly waned: "undergone an eclipse," writes Gustaf Sobin, and thereby "deprived us of our most privileged form of address."

Yet Sobin passionately insists that what hasn't vanished

is the need—call it psychic imperative—that such an address exists. Long after the addressee has vanished, after the omniscient mirror has dissolved and its transcendent dimension has been dismantled, demystified, deconstructed, there remains that psychic imperative deeply inscribed within the innermost regions of our being. We can't do, it would seem, without something that isn't.[11]

For writers, this inability to "do without something that isn't" clashes with a desire (and impotence) to express desire (and impotence) in words.

Why in words?

It is words that sing, they soar, they descend . . . I bow to them . . . I love them, I cling to them, I run from them, I bite into them, I melt them down . . . I love words so much . . . The unexpected ones

. . . The ones I wait for greedily or stalk until, suddenly, they drop
. . . Vowels I love . . . They glitter like colored stones, they leap like
silver fish, they are foam, thread, metal, dew . . . I trap them, clean
them, peel them, they are crystalline texture to me, vibrant, ivory,
vegetable, oily, like fruit, like algae, like agates, like olives . . . And
then I stir them, I shake them, I drink them, I gulp them down, I
mash them, I garnish them, and then I let them go . . . Everything
exists in the word . . .[12]

So wrote Neruda, avowing that words don't merely describe but ac-
tively create existence. John Bierhorst observes,

The belief that words in themselves have the power to make things
happen —especially words in extraordinary combinations—is one of
the distinguishing features of native American thought; and it may
be said that for the people who share this belief a connection ex-
ists between the sacred and the verbal, or to put it in more familiar
terms, a connection between religion and poetry . . . Not surprising-
ly, the word "poetry," as it is understood in English today, has no pre-
cise equivalent in native American languages. What are thought of
by outsiders as Indian "poems" are actually spells, prayers, or words
to songs. Though often appreciated as beautiful, they are seldom
recited purely for entertainment. Rather, they are used for gaining
control or for making things turn out right.[13]

But haven't many generations passed since that belief corre-
sponded with the reality of people?

If Prado's vision longs for that equivalence of religion and poetry,
is her longing outdated—too primitive, too elementary in today's
complex world?

I think not.

★

What strikes me most about Prado is how *present,* how immedi-
ate, is her ability to clash a lofty voice and spiritual concerns with

earthy, sensual vocabulary and tonality. This saves her from a desire to preach, a desire that has destroyed numerous other devotional poets.

Ezra Pound repeated many times that when attacked with questions such as "What do you believe in?" one should answer, "Beauty."

I asked Prado's translator, Ellen Doré Watson, "What is Prado's idea of beauty?

She responded, "Dona Armanda's basket of fruit!"[14]

So, here is a poet who is able to take the language of the senses, of fruit, of bodily, sexual love, and make it the work of religious devotion.

Consider, once more, these lines:

Jonathan wants to see me,
so he will.
The Devil howls, handcuffed down in hell,
while I
tear my body from my clothes.

How far can religion stand from poetry? Does it matter, if such desperate passion surprises the words?

Cioran comes to mind again: "When we are a thousand miles away from poetry, we still participate in it by that sudden need to scream—the last stage of lyricism."[15]

NOTES

Unless noted below, quotations of Prado's poems in the foreword are from this book.

1. Fernando Pessoa, in the guise of his heteronym Alberto Caeiro, from "If they want me to be a mystic, fine. I'm a mystic," section XXX of *The Keeper of Sheep,* in *Poems of Fernando Pessoa,* translated and edited by Edwin Honig and Susan M. Brown (Ecco Press, 1986).

2. E. M. Cioran, *The New Gods,* translated by Richard Howard (University of Chicago Press, 2013).

3. From "Consecration," in the previous selected poems of Adélia Prado, also translated by Ellen Doré Watson: *The Alphabet in the Park* (Wesleyan University Press, 1990).

4. "Denouement," in *The Alphabet in the Park.*

5. From a 2010 interview with Ramon Mello in the Brazilian journal *Saraiva.* See www.saraivaconteudo.com.br/Entrevistas/Post/10483/.

6. For the interview with Ellen Doré Watson in *BOMB* magazine, see http://bombsite.com/issues/70/articles/2289/.

7. Also from Ellen Doré Watson's *BOMB* interview with Prado.

8. Czeslaw Milosz, from *The Witness of Poetry: The Charles Eliot Norton Lectures* (Harvard University Press, 1984).

9. Yehuda Amichai, "God's Hand in the World," from *Selected Poetry of Yehuda Amichai,* translated by Chana Bloch and Stephen Mitchell (University of California Press, 1976).

10. "Dysrhythmia," in *The Alphabet in the Park.*

11. Gustaf Sobin, from *Collected Poems* (Talisman House, 2010).

12. Pablo Neruda, from *Memoirs,* translated by Hardie St. Martin (Farrar, Straus and Giroux, 2001).

13. John Bierhorst, *The Sacred Path: Spells, Prayers & Power Songs of the American Indians* (Harper Perennial, 1984).

14. See "The Mystical Rose," in this book.

15. E. M. Cioran, "Atrophy of Utterance," from *All Gall is Divided: Aphorisms,* translated by Richard Howard (Arcade, 1999).

 The Pelican

It is good for me that I have been afflicted.
—*Psalms* 119:71

Fibrillations

Funeral or feast
no matter which
everything beating inside me
is desire.
O heart that never tires of the resonance of things,
I love, love you, love you,
sad as you are, O world,
O man so handsome that I'm paralyzed.
I love you, I love you.
And with only one tongue,
one sense of pitch, imperfect.
I love you.
There's a certain wild herb with jagged
fuzzy leaves—
I love you, I say, desperate
for a different word to come to my aid.
To the trembling grasses,
love is a breeze.

Lily-Like

Lilies, lilies,
life is all mystery.
I ruin the lilies,
they confuse me.
They blanket the departed,
heaven's flowerbeds
where virgins stroll.
Like heads of garlic,
their bulbs sit beneath the ground
waiting for November to make me suffer.
They grow thick, like people:
Easter lily, water lily, purple lily,
yellow lily—anti-lily—
lily of nothing, spirit of flower,
floral breath of the world,
unfinished thought of God
on this October afternoon I ask myself:
What are lilies for
but to torment me?
A black lily is impossible.
Innocent and voracious, lilies don't exist
and all this talk is delirium.

The Mystical Rose

The first time
I was conscious of form,
I said to my mother:
"Dona Armanda has a basket in her kitchen
where she keeps tomatoes and onions"
and so began fretting that even lovely things
don't last forever,
until one day I wrote:
"It was here in this room that my father died,
here that he wound the clock
and rested his elbows
on what he thought was a windowsill
but was the threshold of death."
I saw that words grouped a certain way
made it possible to live without
the things they described,
my father was coming back, indestructible.
It was as if someone painted a picture
of Dona Armanda's basket and said:
"Now you can eat the fruit."
There was order in the world
—where did it come from?
And why does order—which is joy itself,
and bathes in a different light
than the light of day—
make the soul sad?
We must protect the world
from time's corrosion, we must cheat time itself.
And so I kept writing:
"It was here in this room that my father died . . .

O Night, come on down,
your blackness can't erase this memory."
That was my first poem.

The Sphinx

Ofélia's hair is as black
as the day she got married.
She has nine sons, minus the one
who's a homosexual
and another who's into drugs,
the rest are "normal."
She changed her hairdo and got dentures
but kept her waistline
and that air of some-day-I'll-be-happy,
as innocent and wicked as I am,
insisting on understanding
life—Ofélia's and my own.
Even today she walked by in dress pants
on her way downtown.
The *manacá* blossoms were releasing their perfume
as if the world weren't what it is.
Well, you'll say to me. Well, I say. Well, well.
I don't want to tell stories;
stories are the excrement of time.
What I want to say is that we're eternal,
me, Ofélia, and the *manacá*.

The Transfer of the Body

I was in love with love
and waited for it beneath the trees,
virgin among lilies. I held fast.
Now I see it was a dubious fire
I endured.
The same one endured by tough women
before me.
And it wasn't the demons who gave me the halo
that so infuriated my mother.
Mother long dead,
poor mother,
her wedding dress a shroud,
and she didn't have to be so pale,
and it didn't save her to be so temperate.
It was all a mistake, ash
hawked as treasure.
What was in the box was nothing.
The soul, yes, was murky
and no one could see it.

God Does Not Reject the Work of His Hands

Useless, the baptism of the body,
the efforts of doctrine to consecrate us,
don't eat, don't drink, don't wiggle your hips,
because these are not sins of the body.
The soul, yes, baptize it, confirm it,
expose it to *The Imitation of Christ*.
The body has no black holes,
only innocence and beauty,
so much so that God imitates us
and wants to marry His church
and declares that her "breasts
are like twin gazelles."
Useless, the baptism of the body.
That which has laws obeys them.
The eyes will see God.

Object of Affection

What I have to tell you
is of such high order and so precious
that if I kept it to myself
it would feel like stealing:
the asshole is beautiful!
Make what you will of this gift.
As for me—grateful
to know this,
I feel not forgiveness but love.

Responsory

Saint Anthony,
please find my lost wallet,
you who are tireless,
there with God enjoying your just rewards.
There's a month's pay in that wallet,
plus my I.D.'s and a photo
of me, exhausted, a face
no one would look at twice
except for you, since even when you were here
you had compassion for human anguish:
the disappearing embroidery needle,
boyfriend gone without a trace,
ship on the high seas,
money into thin air.
I have a shopping list, bills to pay,
dues for living on this tumultuous planet.
I promise I'll light a fancy candle,
give a third of my paycheck
pray a third of the rosary,
intoning your praises, O Hammer of Heretics,
whose tongue remained fresh
among your bones, intact.
Servant of the Lord, please find my lost wallet
and if God doesn't think this best for my soul
then teach me instead
to live like you,
like a poor wretch of God,
Amen!

Eternal Life

Half a century.
The weight of that word used to send me straight to bed.
No more. I'm gathering wisdom.
Alchemists aren't law-breakers—
sure, they're naive sometimes, like the saints,
believing in stones, fish seen in dreams,
signs written on the sky.
Where is God?
April is reborn out in the cosmos,
in the most perfect silence.
Inside and outside of me.

Sleeping Beauty

I'm happy—and the reason
secretly borders on humiliation,
because at fifty
I can no longer take a dance class,
choose a profession,
learn to swim like I should.
Meanwhile, I don't know whether it's because of this rain,
the air drawing winged ants out of the ground,
or because he's come back
and turned everything archaic, like the stuff of the soul:
if you go to the meadow,
if you look at the sky,
those tart little fruits,
that tiny new star,
you know nothing has changed.
Papa is alive and coughing,
Mama is cursing sweetly in the kitchen.
As soon as it's dark I'll go out and flirt.
What a good and orderly world!
Flirt with who?
My soul was born wed
to an invisible husband.
When he speaks, dew appears;
I sense his approach
because the grasses bow down.
I'm so attentive that I sleep
more each year.
I swear, under oath:
I'm eighteen. Not even.

Heraldry

What huge luxury to be poor by choice,
temptation to be God who has nothing,
immeasurable pride.
Which is why I'm reminded
that many will enter the Kingdom before me:
thieves, bad poets,
and, worse, the flunkeys who praise them.
I'm distressed by the thought
that kings belong in palaces
and workers in factories and warehouses.
A stiff sentence awaits
those who, like me,
are dazzled by a light so bright!
I know a bad line when I see one,
when it doesn't come straggling
from the unknown margins of the soul.
Is it pride that possesses me
or joy—unrecognizable,
masquerading in rags?
All I know is it's love that fuels
this wearisome task of searching for pearls,
tracing a millennial lineage in coats of arms.
No one knows how to talk about the poor.

The Birth of the Poem

What exists are things,
not words. That's why
I'll tirelessly listen as you recite poems in Bulgarian,
just as I'll spend hours staring at mountains
or clouds.
Signs stand for words,
words stand for things,
things stand for nothing.
Understanding comes like rapture,
it's the same as not understanding.
When my mother lay dying, even my weeping
contained a rainbow:
black will highlight my fair hair.
Granite, gravestone, crepe—
beautiful things or beautiful words?
Marble, sun, cellar door.
Understanding steals me away from words and things
and flings me into the heart of poetry.
That's why I write poems,
to hide what threatens my fatal weakness.
I refuse to believe that people invented languages,
it's the Spirit driving me,
wanting to be adored.
He whispers this hymn in my ear:
buckets, brooms, debts, and fear,
the desire to see Jonathan and be condemned to hell.
I didn't build the pyramids. I am God.

Two o'Clock in the Afternoon in Brazil

As dearly as I love life, I love this heat,
this metaphysical clarity,
this small miracle:
even a scorching sun can't parch these silken petals,
innocent and calm as the young Maccabeans singing in the furnace.
It's my own heart that's suffering,
at two o'clock in the afternoon I need to pray.
Is it God who's calling?
Is it His centrifugal eye exerting its pull?
Life is short and still I haven't found a "style,"
words like astrolabe divert me from my obligations.
The shape of a nose can possess me for weeks,
his sad way of closing his mouth.
Who do I love, after all?
Was I seduced by the Son of Man—
and now confuse stingy you,
conceited you,
with the One who wants me with him
moaning on his bed, his cross?
The European said he was stunned by how much sun we waste here.
Thank you, I replied, embarrassed by *Carnaval,*
Afro-Brazilian drumming, my own extravagant hips.
Is Jesus Bulgarian? Afghani? Dutch?
A Brazilian He's not. He's way foreign,
with his naked, perforated body,
begging for affection, just as I do.
We have folklore, like any country,
and songs dripping melancholy.
But how can I accept that we're going to die?
And the peoples' soul, what good is it?

Meat lockers are horrible
but it's my job to poeticize them,
nothing is to escape redemption:
Jibóia Meats
Freshly cut
Prices sweet
I better pray some more, so I don't feel foreign.
"My God, my God, why hast Thou abandoned me?"
"Tell me who You are and who I am."

The Dark of Night

I'm singled out by flashes
embedded in half-sleep,
pre-dawn, Gethsemane hour.
These visions are raw and clear,
sometimes peaceful,
sometimes pure terror
without the bone structure
daylight provides.
The soul descends to hell,
death throws its banquet.
Until everyone else wakes up
and I can doze,
the Devil eats his fill.
Not-God grazes on me.

Nigredo

Mostly, it's at night, when the soul is vigilant
and an eye not of the body keeps watch.
God! I cry into the darkness,
God, O God!
But it's not me crying out,
it's Him calling Himself
with my mouth of fear.
The bottom of the river falls away.
Children, my children,
husband who chose me,
I, I, I,
in all this dark, such raw sun:
"Mama, save some supper for me."
Not even the whole world could cover such nakedness,
nor the sea, nor God who's treating me
as if I were divine.
He's not who they say He is.
He yells, bids me be crazy,
snatches back the delights
that in dreams He allows:
fish studded in rock face—
first made of glass,
then alive, shuddering,
suspended from mother of crystal,
mother of amethyst.
His mouth is dry, He's thirsty.
He wants water, I drink,
He needs to pee, I get up,
walk naked through the house,

Lord have pity.
Humiliation flattens me—
midnight, midlife at the apex:
the grave, the mother, this great darkness is God
struggling to be born from my flesh.

Note: Nigredo is the alchemical term for cleansing by decomposition or putrefaction, the first step on the pathway to the Philosopher's Stone; Jung interpreted nigredo as a moment of maximum despair that is a prerequisite to personal development.

The Good Shepherd

Let me be leaden,
I don't have a shred of courage left.
I can't have or be
or live or die,
I can neither go in or out.
When I clamor for God, He sends me back to time,
to receipts which
—by order of the government—
I must demand of shady shopkeepers.
Why all this weight on my shoulders?
I didn't ask to be the inspector of the world,
I want to sin, to be free,
leave the thieves
to their tax obligations.
Everything is forbidden,
there's nowhere for me to be,
it's as if God's smacking me around,
pushing me away—
and if asking for help is a sin,
then not asking is insane,
the same as accepting help from the Devil.
Who is this stranger I call Jonathan?
Good God, who am I?
Scorpius is high in the sky—
in happier days I'd write a line:
"The blaze of Scorpius in the chill of night."
Now, it just sounds like flattery,
the words of a liar,
a windbag coward.
You won't believe this

—if you think you're reading a poem—
but someone just handed me a letter:
"I had dentures put in today,
and I do look younger,
but the old-person weariness persists."
And my terror vanished—
because in quoting the letter
I corrected two words,
and no one at the gates of hell
looks to grammar for help.
Thus once more I'm saved by a power,
a compassion
employing the constellations, the mail,
and the same mother tongue
that taught me to wail.
The Merciful One has laid across his shoulders
His weakest lamb.

Divine Wrath

Three days after I was wounded
—who knows whether
by God, the Devil, or myself—
it was seeing the sparrows again
and the little clumps of clover
that told me I hadn't died.
When I was young, those sparrows
and lush leaves alone were enough
for me to sing praises,
dedicate operas to the Lord.
But a dog who's been beaten
is slow to go back to happy barking
and fussing over his owner
—and that's an animal, not a person
like me who can ask:
Why do you beat me?
Which is why, despite the sparrows and the clover,
a subtle shadow still hovers over my spirit.
Whoever hurt me, forgive me.

The Holy Face

Your false teeth are stuck? Pray!
Promise abstinence for a year
to get those cheap things out of your mouth.
O God, You're so good to us—
roses, removable dentures,
tufts of grass like tiny palm trees,
a profusion of miracles.
The poet Casimiro de Abreu, who was no saint
but appeared in our schoolbooks,
used to say, just like Job,
(and my mother and father):
"A Being we cannot see
is greater than the fearsome sea . . . "
What do I do now, as I discover You in silence
but also inside me, in my bones,
dizzying sweetness?
Dentists are the ones who make dentures, not You,
the earth is what brings forth roses.
Ever since I was a girl I've been asking to see You,
show me Your face.
So, this is the splendor,
this desert blazing bright,
too bright to see the way!
This new sweetness depletes me,
like being born fatherless, motherless,
object of a love conceived inside myself.
A flower isn't God, nor is the earth, and me, neither.
Poor and worthless I surrender to whatever it is,
this force of pardon and repose,
infinite patience.
I can almost say I love.

The Battle

I lost my fear of myself. Bye-bye.
I'm off to colder climes, after Jonathan.
This is how we should live:
intoxicated by flight
on a course to certain death.
I love Jonathan.
There you have it: the monotonous, diarrheal subject.
"He wants to see you," said a voice in a dream.
And thus were unleashed the forms in which God hides.
You could worship tufts of grass, sand,
and not discover where oboes come from.
Jonathan wants to see me,
so he will.
The Devil howls, handcuffed down in hell,
while I
tear my body from my clothes.

Ardent Memory

Handsome and mute, he appears
in a thicket of *murici*.
It's the body's high summer,
a season extended by resins.
Like someone training to see God,
I look at the curve of his lip, his forehead,
the prominent nose.
He never says goodbye.
When he leaves I don't notice,
exhausted by such abundance:
his fingers have fingernails—incredible!

The Third Way

Jonathan betrayed me with a woman
who didn't suffer for him
one third as much as I have,
some silly tourist romping around Europe.
Jonathan is so dumb.
I don't know if I should find someone more wily
or wait for him to grow up.
Without my having to get unmarried or spend a dime,
a local guy inspires me daily,
with irresistible possible dangers:
I could catch T.B.,
I could get fat,
I could study physics,
I could fast,
calling up his image at the hottest hour of the day.
Ismália says: "God is a brick,
right here on my dog's nose.
I'm pure sin,"
and then scarfs a bowl of rice pudding
with quiet certainty:
"God loves me, so I will be saved."
I don't have the nerve
to approach God up close like Ismália,
that's why I just yelp,
and approach men up close.
I smell Pedro's shirt,
Jonathan's bitter aftertaste.
When he said pleased to meet you, everyone saw
how my mouth got all dry, and I fainted in my chair.
Love embarrasses me.
I'm from the *cachaça* generation,

either you do or you don't,
you're a housewife or go to the convent,
I can't be gay, can't say, hmmm, it depends,
let's give that a teensy bit of thought.
With me it's wild parties
or strict piety.
I didn't deserve to be born,
to eat with a mouth, walk on two feet
and carry inside me twenty-five feet of guts
all of which desire the filigree of your iris
whose color I keep to myself so as not to ruin everything
and end up utterly ridiculous again.
I now know, and it cost me,
why the saints levitate.
Without a body, the soul has no pleasure.
That's why Christ suffered His passion bodily.
I adore Christ on the Cross.
My desire is atomic,
my fingernail is like my sex.
My foot desires you, my nose.
My spirit—the breath of God in me—desires you,
to do who knows what.
Not kiss or hug, much less marry
and have a heap of kids.
I want you in front of me, motionless—
Saint Francis and the Seraph ablaze—
and me forever and always
looking, looking, looking.

Sketchbook

Who really cares
how crushed I was by the oracle's answers?
Four times I asked, Does he love me?
The answers: silence, conflict,
misfortune, and silence again.
Can Your love, O God, be that beautiful,
You who have neither hands nor feet,
nor that perfect nose
for which I burn to the last star?
If only Jonathan loved me . . .
But the one who loves me is João,
even though I've loved Jonathan since age twelve,
since my one happy memory of Sister Guida
who taught drawing class—
shapes were a welcome escape from doctrine,
forms more ancient than Papa and Mama,
more ancient even than Grandpa,
demanding I do something
so they would last, stay there with me in my sketchbook.
I drew without relish,
poking the paper with my pencil,
aiming—I now know—
(and wish I didn't)
to cast out that mortal beauty.
I was wrestling with the Angel,
the Messenger who would never again leave me.
How can something immortal have a name?
God's name is anything at all,
since even when he doesn't answer
joy appears like dew.

Syllabication

The hole where the tooth was
and the space from there to the red star above the river
both contain airplanes and questions.
People are passing judgment
on my dress and hair
while I write a book
which, according to my sister-in-law,
"leaves behind many memories."
My hayseed looks
rattled a refined young man
and I endured many moments
with my mother bedeviling my ear:
"You're scrubbing your feet for nothing,
that Notajan or whatever his name is
will marry some rich girl for sure."
I'd rather he hated me
than to hear that beloved name
massacred in her mouth.
O Jonathan, words kill me,
the perfect and the raw ones.
Corn, coffee, kitchen soap,
my poor mother prepared me for life,
this vale of tears.
Vale of tears! What a fantastic word!
If I knew how, I'd say it
in every language on the planet,
Vale of tears!
All of humanity's eyes emptying,
to fill ravines between cliffs,
entire canyons,

creating an ocean,
bitter and salty.
Ocean, no. More like a river,
because Vale of Tears
is not as desperate or immense
as the sea.
A river has banks,
land stretching out
with plants, animals, keepers of cattle.
A cry can be heard.

Crazy Behavior

The temptation to reject form insinuates itself
and I can't tell whether from Good or Evil.
A weariness with anything that's revealed
through the power of words arranged
one certain way and no other.
That's when I'm most certain I'm not God.
Jonathan, Jonathan,
My mother can't say your name right,
her hate discombobulates the syllables
and even more so the motives
for her woeful warnings.
I too want to overstep.
Lovers suffocate cacophony,
admiring the body's boisterous machine.
—Papa, did you sleep well?
Oh, yes! He'd say,
then innocently mention crowing roosters,
newborns shrieking in the night.
But the pleasure of his details!
If my mother's right, I'm sunk.
I've always claimed that poetry is God's footprint on things
and sung its praises,
when it's His feet we should adore.
Poetry is a shackled servant,
a blind bird trilling,
such meager beauty.
Meanwhile it is written: "You are gods!"
And we are.
I want to offer myself to the divine
in the most perfect poverty

but the divine will only accept me
in the most perfect joy.
Inside the lit light bulb
the nucleus looks like an egg yolk,
a brand-new chick.
I have to lie a little bit
to get the rhythm going
—or even just to understand.
A longing wells up, unrelenting,
for the one who inhabits my chest:
Come, Jonathan,
bring flowers for my mother
and a pair of hand-cuffs for me.

Furious with Jonathan

I went looking for you in the street,
knocked my head on a lamppost,
bled, sobbed, slept,
and dreamed of heavenly bodies stirring,
humanoid trees.
The body is pagan and should stay that way,
a constant reminder to God
of his duty to save us.
Cruel and mortal man,
I'm disgusted by the arpeggio of liquids
in your pale abdomen.
Beat it, you imbecile dog,
you're going to go hungry today,
that bone is mine.
Bad company is ruining you, my love,
depleting you of your power to write good poems.
You get distracted, you forget about me,
give uppity interviews.
An egg with two yolks
would move the coldest person,
but not me, not today,
I don't even want to hear about Greek art.
I draw badly, it's true,
but why should Sister Guida
show off at my expense?
If Brígida provokes me,
I'm going to respond like a doctor:
"Brígida, it's your unconscious that produces bad behavior."
Only this will humiliate her enough,
and wash the phlegm from these horrendous lines:

"Florid, feverish, blushing,
  my feminine honor convulsing,
  this cyclical, periodic passion drums
  in my chest, ultra-sonic."
  Scram, you travesty of a poem. Good gracious!
  But, as I was saying,
  come, Jonathan,
  anytime is the right time,
  what matters is to be happy,
  a bird in the hand is worth more—
  come, my gallant!—than two in the air,
  but pray come soon, you scoundrel,
  or I'll drill you full of holes,
  I don't give a hoot.
  I'll be wearing a wedding dress
  and holding forth, a head of cabbage in my hand:
"Dear people, most excellent citizens . . . "
  Jonathan, you'll look so fine in your coffin!
  Only one tiny thing holds me back—
  if I commit the crime,
  what will happen later
  whenever I come across a safety pin
  with its ungrateful, super-humble, ultra-useful form?
  And who will trust the word of Isaiah
  who wrote his prophesies for me?
"Make firm the feeble knees. . .
  the lame shall leap like deer."
  Hmmm, Jonathan? Answer me.

The Sacrifice

Neither sea nor political storm
nor ecological disaster
could keep me from Jonathan.
Twenty winters would not be enough
to make his image fade.
Morning, noon, night,
like a diamond
my love perfects itself, indestructible.
I sigh for him.
Getting married, having children—
all just pretense, diversion,
a human way to give me rest.
There are days when all I want is to avenge myself,
blurting curse words: damn, damn,
but it's myself I damn,
since this love lives inside me
and maybe it's only God playing the mime.
I want to see Jonathan
just as fervently
as I want to kneel down and worship
and belt out the "Panis Angelicus."
I've been singing since childhood.
Since childhood I've desired and still desire
the presence that would silence me forever.
While the other girls danced,
I stood still, wanting,
I lived on wanting.
Pomegranate liqueur,
invisible blood pulsing in the presence Most Holy.
Lustily, I sing out:
Jonathan is Jesus.

The Pelican

One day I saw a ship up close.
I stared for a long time
with the same slow greed that I watch Jonathan:
fingernails first, then fingers, knuckles.
I loved that ship.
Oh! I said. What a thing is a ship!
It swayed gently back and forth,
smooth as a seducer.
I looked around for someone, longing to say:
Look! Look—a ship!
Eager to talk about what I didn't understand
so as to learn at last
how something with no feet
walks on the wide waters.
One night before sleep—
just as I'd seen the ship—I saw a feeling.
Beset by oohs and aahs, sudden muteness,
almighty vocatives, I stammered:
Oh, you! And O You!
—my throat burning to cry.
It struck me that there in the dark of night
I was poeticized,
desired by supreme desire.
O Mercy, I said,
and placed my mouth on the torrent from His chest.
O love, and I let Him caress me,
as the vision faded,
lucid, illogical,
true as a ship.

Silly Girl

I want to see Jonathan,
here or wherever he lives
exiled from me.
It's a drizzly Sunday
like the one long ago
when Ormírio arrived
with his step-daughter, Antonia,
and gave me a bunch of grapes.
I feel the same kind of longing
for that Sunday as I feel for Jonathan.
Antonia was as simple as I was happy,
the earth was spinning slowly on its axis,
and everything conspired
to make me sing my favorite song.
When I fell in love with Jonathan,
I wrote his name all over the house,
and my father asked: "What's this?"
The name of a prince, I told him,
it's pronounced Narratanói—
it's from the Thousand and One Nights . . .
My rough-hewn father,
easily humbled by certain words,
was proud of me
for giving him power over phrases from afar.
Oh, Jonathan, I discover that I've loved you
since WWII
when the allies were beating the Germans.
Grandpa used to pronounce it "theeallies,"
and Mama, too, imagine!
And me more than anyone:

"Theeallies are going to win the war."
Because I knew by divine inspiration:
"Power belongs to he who has dominion over words."
I planned to use this power against you,
which my mother had used against me:
"You're working class,
he's too handsome,
he'll leave you in the end!"
But, Mama, he didn't, just as my vocation for perfect joy
won't desert me,
despite all the sorrows.
Look, decades later,
and still intact:
my eagerness for rain,
for green guavas,
and sun that illuminates roof tiles
with the white flames of noon.
It's as if she were still here
with Papa, Grandpa,
Ormírio and the bunch of grapes,
like when I burst out with "Tantum Ergo,"
the wrong song for Christmas Eve.
What a great courtesan I was practicing to be,
because it was an orgy,
that happiness made of trifles,
it was all so shabby.
I was already in love with Jonathan,
because Jonathan is this:
a poetic fact that has always existed,
dream-matter, dreams themselves,
where everything else becomes unimportant.
Now that I've decided to be a mystic,
I write on his picture:

"Jesus, José, Jehovah, Jonathan, Jonathan,
the smallest flower is my judge.
Leave me in the desert atoned,
stone made of stone yet
set upon stone."
I rhyme for prettiness, it's not that I'm feeling sad.
You could call this poem "Tortured Girl,"
but meanwhile, I certify that I'm happy,
glad to have squandered
what I meant to ration,
which—it's certain—
time does not erode.
Honey flows,
a sweet songbird feeds me.
Lightning against black sky
and this sweetness that never rests.
Even more so than the flowers,
these vegetables are made for me,
my belly converts them into symbolic gold.
Nothing comes close to what I am
except another person and another
and yet another person.
I see a newborn baby and I'm transported.
I try saying: "Inside the earth,
sheets of water over beds of sand."
It's like plunging a spear in my chest,
I vibrate, loving the torrent
as I love Jonathan.
Fish are fond of me, and fetuses.
I embrace people before they embrace me,
I disarm them,
tenacious as a bee
I try to make them understand:

Life is so good,
all it takes is one kiss
for the delicate gears to get moving,
a cosmic necessity protects us.
The unclean spirits proclaimed the Christ
as they entered the swine.
This new joy is proclaiming me,
the same joy
as long ago when I was given grapes and it was raining
and I was happy to see Antonia,
that silly girl.
"Wrath sits ready to ambush like a sharp-toothed fish"
is nothing but a pretty line.
There's no returning from this country:
a man at the window sings—
unrehearsed—a little melody.
God placed the rainbow in the sky,
and branded it,
His hieroglyph.
I'm out of time,
happiness consumes me.

Knife in the Chest

The human heart—dark, dark.
— João Guimarães Rosa,
from *Grande Sertão: Varedas*

Biography of the Poet

Once there was a house with *copaíba* trees,
                two huge ones.
And so begins my love for Jonathan,
with this beautiful account.

Each time my father mentioned the *copaíbas*,
it was as if to report anew:
"God spoke to Moses from these very trees."
Well then. Two *copaíbas*,
two o'clock in the afternoon,
everyone making coffee.
A voice announced:
"You and your brother can play right here,
                you won't be in the way."
Anyone who could rhyme was called a poet.
The world beckoned,
                flowers down here,
                stars up above.
Not even Solomon in his glory
                was happier.
Can the horror of feces be turned to love?
Must I experience at least minimal
discomfort and strangeness
                in order to remain human?
I wanted to invent the cross-stitch and yeast
(it's humiliating to follow recipes),
                tiny butterflies, computers,
                narrow streams full of fish,

telegraph cables under the sea.
I discover that I've never seen
        the true Face of God.
There are women in my circle
        who pray joylessly
and can recite the entire book from top to bottom,
including the copyright, list of editions, preface,
and address to report answered prayers.
All I want is to say: O Beauty, I adore You!
My entire body trembles at Your look.

The Meticulous One

The cerebral poet takes his coffee without sugar
and retires to his office to concentrate.
His pencil is a scalpel
      sharpened on stone,
the calcinated stone of words—
an image chosen because he loves difficulty
      and the respect that comes
of his contract with the dictionary.
Three hours he's been trying to incite the muses.
The day blazes on. His balls itch.
Meanwhile, in no time at all
things will begin to phosphoresce in the forest.
God's servant leaves her cell nightly
      and walks down the road,
because God feels like a stroll
and she can walk.

And the young poet,
      reeking of suicide and glory,
steals from all of us: "God is impeccable"
      —and doesn't even need to sign his name.
Frogs startle and leap,
      but the meticulous one doesn't get it;
he wants to write things with words.

Laetitia Cordis

Settle down a minute and look, a miracle:
cloud-covered morning,
touch of chill and fog.
My heart, yellow as a *pequi* fruit
        beats like this:

        Jonathan, Jonathan, Jonathan.
        All around me they're saying:

"It's just haze, the sun's sure to come out."
        I'm thinking about Giordano Bruno
and what an incredible lover he'd be.
I want to dance
and watch a Slavic film—without subtitles,
so I can guess when those strange sounds
        are saying I love you.
People are so beautiful,
        God is so handsome.
I am Jonathan, leaning against my bicycle,
        posing for a picture.

When the *pequi* are ripe
        they split open and fall,
making nests on the ground, yolk-yellow.

My heart wants to leap,
to beat here on the outside,
        like His.

History

It afflicts me to read:
"The first bicycles appeared in eighteen-hundred-and-something."
I need them to be eternal. God understands,
God and anyone who reads poems the way I think of Jonathan.
My father said:
"Grandpa would tell how his great-great-grandfather
rode around on a funny bicycle delivering cheeses,
also eternal, and eggs,
which have always existed.
He had the same last name you do,
                    my daughter,
which he gave to his son, who would give it to his grandson,
a cord planted in the belly button of our Eternal Father."
Which is why I'm in no danger of not meeting Jonathan,
joy of my life for whom I wait like in the Psalm,
"more eagerly than the night guard awaits the dawn."
Human history is picturesque. Dates
                  are scholars' toys.
When God created the world
he created the bicycle and the green path
where Jonathan waits for me, for this beautiful scene:
as the lovers pass by,
                the flowering grasses shiver.

Immolation

A heat wave is revving in my body,
sign of the cycling down
of something in me
                    that will never again
        be rose or satin.
Meanwhile, compared to dried flowers
and old photographs—laughable today—
these remain unchanged:
shoals of fish, corollas,
new shoots dancing in the afternoon breeze.
How are such tiny fish possible,
and this yellow—or any yellow at all?
Fish live underwater
                    and they don't drown!
Take my life, I have yet to ask God,
                to prove the measure of my joy.
Today what I want is to laugh at this silly contrivance:
                "a wagonload of devils."
Wagons are peaceable things
and a little yelling would drive away devils like those.
In the root of sadness, this antibody:
whatever it is yellow is,
that's what my soul and its happiness are made of—
and the world's beauty and Christ's soul.

Opus Dei

Butterflies never give up,
they have no idea their name is unbecoming.
The seasons follow each other flawlessly
and still you're afraid to admit
       there's no sin in saying
O Beauty, thou art my joy.
Loosen up,
       Jonathan is just a man.
If you so much as curl your lip
his lance retreats.
Insects are beyond understanding,
wisely gnawing on precious treatises.
One drop of sap can kill a man.
That's why you should surrender to anything
that makes you that beautiful when you laugh.
          This is not comic opera.
It's just a not-knowing shot through with lightning.
       If Jonathan turns out to be God, you're right
       and if not, you're still right
       because you believe it
and no one can be blamed for loving.

In Portuguese

Spider, cork, pearl
and four more that I won't tell
are perfect words.
Dying is unsurpassable.
God weighs nothing.
Butterflies is *seilfrettub,*
soap boiling in the pot.
I hope these oddities
are psychologisms,
corruptions owing to
original sin.
Words—I want them first as things.
My head is getting tired
                of this unhappy discourse.
Jonathan asked:
            "Have you had your yoghurt today?"
What sweetness spilled over me, such comfort!
Languages are imperfect
                so that poems can exist,
and so I can ask where do these come from—
winged insects and this tenderness,
his arm grazing mine.

Parameter

God is better-looking than I am.
And He's not young.
That's consolation.

Words and Names

I'm equally dumbfounded by mystics
and by clothing stores with their prices.
My tooth is rotting
and I won't lift a finger to save it,
having chosen fear
                as my lord and master.
There's dust to spare on the bookshelf
                and books in overabundance
and letters all full of themselves blocking the way:
"To me, writing is a religion."
Writers are unbearable,
                except for the sacred ones,
who put "Oracle of the Lord" at the end.
I feel paralyzed
because I want fire like that—
and well-cut clothes
                made of imported fabric.
Ai! I'm never going to write a "Cantar D'Amigo."
But meanwhile, as if I were Galician,
doves coo in my soul,
in the eaves, in early morning,
                sparrows, little seamstresses.
Now my name is none,
unlike the many encrusted in my old one:
Délia, Adel, Élia and Lia,
and to my affliction
Leda, Lea, Dália,
Eda, Ieda and also Aia.
Aia is the best!
Aia, servant of a noblewoman,
        a lady-in-waiting,

whose job it is
        to record her life on paper
and spy m'lady through a peep hole
having sex with the King.
Butterfly—both the spelling
        and the sound are mistakes
and mistakes interest me,
I kill spiders to learn
                where they come from.
Nature is obedient and happy,
nature follows its own laws,
        it doesn't flow from God.
But me—what am I?

The Tenacious Devil Who Doesn't Exist

God's glory is greater
                    than this plane in the sky.
And his love,
            which is where my fear comes from,
that sea of delights
            where planes crash
            and ships founder,
I know oh so well,
and I also know how disastrous it is
            to be the body of time,
                            to exist,
such intermittent terror.
Jonathan, if death is love
                    then why
—if I'm so certain—am I still afraid?
How can a fish be happy when I'm not?
Strange, this business of being human.
One evening, I opened the door
and there was a toad
                    with this throbbing gullet,
            a gentle toad.
And I thought: it's Jonathan in disguise
                    come to visit me.
Even so, I shooed him away with a broom
                            and went to watch television.
Under a starry sky,
        I lay sleepless, astonished.
God's love and His Beauty
                    are one in the same.
I want to be holy like Agnes

who flies on the wings of beetles
            singing to soothe me
                        with her little girl's voice:
"Cast off the chains
            around your neck,
      O captive daughter of Zion."
      Airplanes are scary
      because God is in them.
Embrace me, God, with Your
                  flesh and blood arm.
      Sing with Your mouth
            to keep me innocent.

Matter

Jonathan has arrived.
And my love for him is so demented
that I forgot about God,
I, who pray day and night.
But I don't want Jonathan to linger,
because I'm in danger
of talking crazy
in front of everyone.
When something wants to happen it begs for a brazen meter,
                                        clamoring to be real.
Centipedes take a stroll on my body.
            He calls me Agnes
            and says un-reproducible things:
"I sense that a small vase
                with three plastic roses
            could flood you with life and death."
            Jonathan, do you exist?

Form

There's only one way to say to someone:
                    "I can't get you out of my head."
The cello string sets itself vibrating
                    beneath an invisible bow
and sins disappear like mice caught in the act.
          My heart is astounding because it beats
          and is filled with blood and is going to stop some day
          and because it becomes a pathetic drum
                    when you whisper in my ear:
                    "I can't get you out of my head."
Splotches of light on the wall,
          a small vase
                    with three plastic roses.
Everything in the world is perfect
          and death is love.

Lighter Than Air

What brought me to Jonathan?
A dream bicycle,
faster than a plane.
Enchanted, it rides on the sea,
leaps mountains,
stops at the flowery gate.
Jonathan is in his office,
      the table lamp glowing.
I hesitate to knock,
giving my heart a chance to quiet.
Jonathan senses my presence
      and yanks the curtain back,
      trying to startle me.
      There are two bicycles on the plain.

Guess

Pick a month,
          I said to the saint.
She chose October.
And the girl I asked, all innocence,
picked October, too.
I'm not asking anyone else,
since that's the month
I plan to chisel the raw gold
                    out of his name.
I was thinking of Jonathan when I rigged
                              this up,
I'm thinking of him now,
               doing what I do best,
sending love notes
with the power of thought:
          Jonathan, listen,
          I'm the fly hovering around you:
          down by the ruins—in October.

One More Time

I don't want to love Jonathan any more.
I'm tired of this love with no coddling and cuddling,
destined to become old-people love.
Oh!—I've never said that before—
                    old-people love.
Fortunately, it's a lie.
Even if Jonathan forgets me
          and this song is played out of tune
like a bad Bolero,
I still want the Holland bicycle
and later the Gothic crypt
where our bones can sleep.
          O Jonathan,
you're not the one who makes
the invisible cornucopia pour out gold.
          Me neither.
I want to uglify the poem
                    to fling my displeasure at you—
                              in vain.
The One who gave me these words is writing this,
with my hand.

Letter

Jonathan,
because of you
things are starting to happen to me.
I'm full of fear.
I want to move away from here.
I'm sick of my family, my work in the parish,
and I've actually pondered
getting my hair done up like certain singers.
I have no patience for news of who died or got married—
and this whole strange cycle began when I met you.
I go without eating for days, I hardly sleep,
rehearsing dialogs for when we meet
in that distant place far from the eyes of Marcionília,
who, completely out of malice, asked why I've been so happy lately.
Tell me what time you think of me,
so I can set my watch for Madagascar time,
where you're managing to resist sending me a postcard.
No one knows about us,
except for Soledade and my dear sister.
I share my delirium only with them.
You could have called, written,
sent a telegram, signs of life.
I'm in danger of getting sick.
I caught myself grunting, kissing my own arm.
I'm truly crazy. From longing. All because of you.
Write to me. Or invent a way—I know a thousand—
to send a message.
I'm standing at the window of the bedroom where I don't sleep,
watching Alpha and Beta—who in my imagination

represent you and me.
Do you think me childish, Jonathan?
They're insisting that I go welcome the Ambassador.
I said no. Spelled it out one letter at a time: n-o.
I told them, just for fun,
that I expect a visitor from Manchuria that very day,
a distinguished professor coming all that way to discover
why I fill so many notebooks with this mirrored code:
UOYEVOLI NAHTANOJ.
I'm hoping a war will break out
so you'll have to immigrate to Arvoredos.
They're inspecting me. I must have been talking too loud.
I kiss your yellow fingernail and your eyes that pretend to be
    distracted
merely to intensify my passion,
I'm sure of it, and still it intensifies.
Alpha, my dear, ciao.

Always Your Beta.

Note from the Daring Damsel

Jonathan,
there are suspicious fascists about.
Put on that shirt I hate
—the one from the Moroccan bazaar—
and come by the house, as if to fix the shower.
Take advantage of Tuesday, when my parents
go to visit Aunt Quita in Lajeado.
If their plans change, I'll send another note.
Don't bring an umbrella—even if it's raining.
I just can't take Uncle Emílio any more,
the way he knows and pretends not to know
I'm seeing you on the sly,
and is forever making up nicknames for you.
What you said the other day at that party at the rancher's
is music playing in my ears, even today:
"I can't stop thinking about you."
Me, too, Natinho, not for a minute.
Tuesday, two p.m.,
if the world ends,

                    I won't even notice.

                            In agony,
                                    Beta

One Thing After Another

As hard as I try,
my handwriting doesn't come out round.
                              God sees me.
I don't write letters any more,
only bad words, on the wall.
                    Fuck you. Die.
I'm tired of saying I love you.
My patience has no beginning and no end.
I never stop thinking about Jonathan.

          I detest elegant writing.
          Tragedies are sweet.
I learned to talk extremely early.
          Everything I say is vanity.
It's impossible to live without saying I,
          word reserved for God.
I don't know how to be human.
One day I will, if Jonathan loves me:
          "What strong fingernails!"
          "You remind me of someone."
          "I almost sent you a postcard."
              Crumbs, Jonathan.
          You're going to die some day, too.
                    Talk to me,
          give my heart some rest.

Marvels

I almost went into ecstasy today,
        wishing so intensely for a miracle:
for this flower to burst into bloom in front of me,
or for the light to blink three times.
And then from nowhere, the thought that I'm living in sin,
            Christ admonishing:
       "He who looks at a woman lustfully
         has already committed adultery in his heart."
But Jonathan isn't a woman
        and who, these days, unless secretly,
follows the Biblical teaching
to whip a misbehaving slave's back
until drawing blood?
O swallow,
perch on my shoulder as a sign.
O Scorpius,
        move your blue tail,
        twirl in the sky, crescent moon.
Tell me, old bible, where is my error?
"How many times did they tempt Him in the desert,
and in solitude afflict Him?"
This beautiful verse
says God "killed the Egyptian first-born males."
"His breath burned like a live coal."
God's law keeps me from Jonathan,
          who brings me closer to God,
       because he's beautiful and he loves me
     and he's not afraid to use his flesh-and-blood lips

to touch mine.
In the good old days, they stoned
adulterers to death.
That which holds the sea within its bounds
cares about the sea.
Why not care about me? I know how to rage, too.
I love God, I love Jonathan.
I love, I love, I love.

Trinity

God gives me nothing but dreams.
He takes away everything else, indifferent to my screams,
because every dream is Him disguised as Jonathan
and his unreachable face made of marble.
My boasting! I never went further than brushing fingers
                                        under the saucer:
More coffee, Jonathan? More coffee?
And he thought me daring because I looked at his shoes,
                        and then right away at the window,
so that, following that oblique line, he would read
                                        the urgency of my soul.
Did he kiss me one day or was that a dream, excessive desire?
God separates me from God, His heart is a furnace
burning with love for me, who burns with love for Jonathan,
who is staring at Orion, impassive as a boulder.
"Be careful, your fantasies might come true."
I imagine saying to Jonathan:
Let me hurt your lip to prove that you exist.
"We must consider the secret judgment of God,"
a light I can barely perceive, shivering in the fog.
Jonathan, who I love, is divine,
but I think he's human too.
One day he's going to take my head in his hands with unexpected
    tenderness.
And then, O God,
almost against my will I'll say:
                        I love you.

The Last Supper

He began by saying: "Love . . ."
but couldn't finish
because someone was calling him.
"Love . . ." as if he were touching me,
  speaking to me only,
  though there were other people at the table.
"Love . . ." and he scraped his chair nearer.
  I didn't raise my eyes, afraid
          of the explicitness of my heart.
  My breath was a crackling fire,
  heating up the room.
"Love . . ."
Just this one word of his unfinished utterance
to nourish the hunger desire perpetuates.
Jonathan is my food.

Pastoral

When it gets to be too much,
   when my longing for Jonathan has me really agitated,
      I go to the country.
      Walking between rows of coffee,
  stalks of corn and lustrous tea leaves,
          his soulful presence calms me.
  He smells of resins,
     sweetness,
hidden in termites, tree bark,
        honey I've never tasted.
My heart pleads for the loving order of the world:
  Come, Jonathan. And a beetle appears
        with his same way of walking.
  I discover that songbirds
         do only what gives them pleasure
      and they urge me on from the bamboo:
Little woman, you too
    should fulfill your destiny.
There's a sacrament called
    The Presence of the Most Holy,
a heart saying the same thing as mine:
       come, come, come.
I've experienced God's wrath,
    and now his watchful jealousy.
Even in the roots of shrubs
—even in things I see and things I don't see,
like the imperceptible paths of ants—

He, Jonathan, and I,
    knife, sweetness, and ecstasy,
pain that never deserts me.

The Hermit's Apprentice

It's very difficult to fast.
I use my mouth to decipher the world,
                    making words,
kissing Jonathan's lips,
                    which call me Primora,
a secret love name he invented.
Mouths play flutes,
the soul is born from the breath of God,
such lovely pain that I ask for more,
just a little bit more.
Please God, don't ask me to return what you've given me.
My body is innocent again,
I love Jonathan like pastures without fences
                    even if he does forget me sometimes.
This here is *murici,* it makes cow's milk smell so sweet!
A herd of butterflies,
a herd of stars in the sky,
created to astonish to my soul.
O beauteous world!
I want to know who made the world
                    so carefully careless.
Parrots' tongues resemble
cashew nuts,
Jonathan's nose, Yours. Perfection plural.
Parrots talk, Jonathan inhales
and from his breath, this sound: Primora.
It was You who loved me first:
"Take, eat."
But wouldn't that mean Your Kingdom is food?
What do I know? I don't know.

But everything is body, even You,
                    measurable matter.
The spirit seeks words,
the blind hear sounds,
the deaf see lights,
the chest thunders, ready to explode.
Hail mysteries! Hail world!
God's body, my mouth,
marvel that I write, at the risk of my life:
I love you, Jonathan,
believing that you're God
and that that word from your mouth will save me.
You welcome me as you do the Aurora Consurgens:
                    Come, Primora.
You talk like a man,
but what I hear is a roar
rushing down from the North Pole.
God. Give me courage to be born.

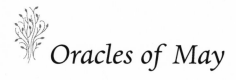 Oracles of May

I want vocatives to call you, O May.

The Poet Wearies

I've had it with being Your herald.
Everybody has a voice,
why am I the one who has to get on board
with no say about where we're headed?
Why not proclaim the wondrous woof of looms
Yourself, with that voice that echoes
to the four corners of the earth?
The world's seen so much progress
and you still insist on traveling salesmen
going door-to-door on horseback.
Check out this jackknife, people,
Take a good look, ma'am, it's magic:
slices and screws, tweezes and dices—
a whole set of tools in one!
Dear God,
let me work in the kitchen.
I'm not a peddler, or a scribe,
just let me make Your bread.
Child, says the Lord,
all I eat is words.

God's Assistant

I invoked the Holy Spirit,
He said: suffer,
eat patiently
this bitterness,

because you have a mouth
and I don't.
Take this tiny chalice,
this bread of gall and ash
untransformed.
It's made of myrrh,
come, eat.

Salve Regina

Melancholia looms.
I want to be joyful
without needing to write,
without thinking
the labor of bees
and the flight of butterflies
must be recorded.
These women bemoaning their marriages—
I knew them years ago
as happy children.
That's life, eh, Lord?
The skin on my face, the skin of my dreams—
are they really collapsing?
But that's not what I'm here to announce—
I can see where these lines are going,
this is a poem, it has rhythm,
it answers to a higher order
and seems to be ignoring me.
Bad dreams arrive:
a house with only one door,
a jail-house,
high walls, narrow rooms.
I call after my husband but he's gone,
he comes back a black man,
and indifferent.
The child who got lost
—or I allowed to get lost in me—
is a wolf-boy,
I discover him grunting,

beside an old black couple.
More blacks—I wonder why?
Why this dream?
I spend hours asking for help,
like a nun outside the convent,
I exhaust myself,
devising silent spaces
in which to discover Your voice.
It's fear that proclaims my love,
this cheerfulness is a recording.
The first Brazilian saint
prayed on behalf of a poor man:
"*Post-partum, Virgo Inviolata permansisti.*
Dei Genitrix, intercede pro nobis."
O Virgin,
Restore my soul to joy,
I too
hold my hand out for alms.

Buried Treasure

Farther away the closer it gets,
time outwits science.
This fossil is how many million years old?
The same age as my pain.
Love laughs at swagger,
men sleepless over their calculators.
The invisible enemy decks himself out
to keep me from saying what makes me eternal:
O world! I've loved you ever since
the unrebellious angels came on the job.
When caught in thoughts that lead nowhere,
salvation comes from saying: I adore You.
Knees on the earth, I adore You,
O gold-bearing mustard seed,
tiny heart in the entrails of minerals.
In mud, feces, and suspicious secretions
I adore You, love You above all things.

Staccato

An ant stops me in my tracks,
"What's your hurry, miscreant, no time to help me?"
But it's not her voice, it's His,
intercepting me,
needy, needy God.
If I don't say: I love You,
His pain will turn us both to ice.

Domus

Eyes set into the ridgepole,
the house peers down at the man.
Such sensitive, discerning walls,
now and then its ears tremble:
love one minute,
invective the next,
then fist-pounding panic.
God is touched
by the house the man has made,
God whose eyes peer down
from the ridgepole of the world.
The house begs mercy for its owner
and his fantasies of good fortune.
It seems impassive, but suffers.
The house is alive and speaks.

A Good Death

Dona Dirce was grieving for her daughter,
weeping real tears,
reaching for the coffee
her other daughter offered.
I watched Dona Dirce listen in amazement
to what Alzirinha was saying:
" . . . and so the doctor expressly forbade me to—"
Someone poked his head in the door looking for Dona Dirce:
"What's the plate number on Artur's pick-up?"
Alzirinha didn't want any coffee cake, she was on a diet,
and was it possible that Artur hadn't heard the news yet?
A freckle-faced teenager was visibly happy,
crying over her mother's death.
I felt like crying, too,
for various other reasons,
but it was impossible there,
they were celebrating life
beneath contrite faces,
beneath mourning veils—
more than seven.
As each veil fell,
death covered herself up,
to protect us:
"More coffee, anyone?"
Death was modest, a consoling companion,
practically a member of the family.
Lucinda had become a saint.
But I didn't tell anyone, so as not to rain on their sadness.

Poem for a Girl Apprentice

It's a desperate day
here in Divinópolis
but my patience will seduce
every last one.
The little girl insists
on tidying the kitchen,
she's like an empress: "Out!"
The serious man attempts flattery:
"I appreciate you even more without glasses."
Hapless fellow.
The councilmen will applaud my remarks
about historical memory,
but if they were to excavate me they'd find nothing
except desire,
almost ungratefulness.
A pilgrimage is about to set out for Congonhas do Campo,
I want to join them,
get some dust under my nails.
"Is there anything else that needs washing up?"
Yes, my own soiled soul—
a grain of hope would wash it clean.
You can go play now, Beatriz.

On Love

In this way you are put to the test,
in the ashes of the obvious,
following behind a leaky truck,
when the man who asked for your hand
proclaims:
"It's carrying liquid."
You're a saint if you say nothing
and set your hand on his knee—
or the queen of hell if you bark:
No kidding, if it's dripping –
what else would it be carrying?
Love is a painful sifting
that produces gold nuggets,
elixirs of long life;
from its little plot of land
springs the tree of perpetual youth.
It's like gardening,
practically immoral to enjoy
the fumes of manure,
a half-good bad smell
(as the boy said of the piglets in their pen).
Love is more than violent.

Portunhol

I'm trying to say
that the body of Your Spirit in the garden
is light without harshness.
Have I said it?
Rose and rosemary
only seem to differ.
A mirror is what I am,
and not always clouded;
those who see themselves in me
judge me merciful.
Understanding
is when the body of light escapes you
and a clarity remains, glowing,
it's when you say:
Amazing! Such delicate weavings on their looms!
Computers know
when I write rose with a "z",
they correct me like teachers.
I'm struck by an overwhelming desire
for pork rinds
and an entire bottle of wine,
life quivering somewhere inside
—only here between my legs, until today—
and I long for *alabanza,*
long to dance to castanets,
and to say all lovely and wrong:
"I feel me this, too."
No one can deny that God is love.

Nap with Flowers

Ofélia thinks a tempest
is a rainstorm with a slow tempo.
It's back, the little taptapping
noise in my ear.
Calling someone a cow is an insult,
but only the word—cows are good.
I suffer from aristrocraticism,
me of all people,
born way out in Rusty Creek.
I invaded my son once,
if I ever do that again
I'll give up my tongue.
At the schoolhouse door
one sick boy helps
another up the steps,
we humans are God's crutches.
There's no rest for us here
in exile,
building mobiles in the sand.
Roosters know,
they crow at all the wrong times
to hurry the day along,
newborns scream
god is god is god is
and then there are the dahlias
smelling of virginity and death.
The taptapping taps on,
but now it's like a lullaby:
god is god is god is

Meditation Verging on a Poem

I pruned the rosebush at the perfect moment
and left town for days,
having learned once and for all
to wait biblically,
everything in its time.
One day I opened the window, and there it was
as I'd never seen it before,
studded
with buds,
some already with that pale rose
peeking out between sepals,
clusters of living jewels.
My bad back,
my disappointment with the limits of time,
my enormous effort to be understood—
all turned to dust
before this recurrent miracle.
The cyclical, perceptible roses
have made themselves marvelous.
No one can dissuade me
from what—beyond the structure of reason—
I knew all at once:
mercy is intact.
Billowing greed,
pummeling fists,
high-pitched fury—
nothing can hold back gold corollas
or—believe me—fragrance.
Because it's springtime.

Mural

At the nest collecting eggs,
the woman
neither young nor old
is perfectly broken in.
The indecisive sun doesn't cast
this expansive light,
it's she who gives birth
to nature's veiled radiance,
it's her own delight
in having a family,
loving her agreeable routine.
She doesn't know she knows
the perfect routine is God:
the hens lay their eggs,
she lays out her skirt,
the tree in due season
displays those rosy blossoms.
The woman doesn't know she's praying:
Lord, let nothing change.

Our Lady of the Conception

I'm ten years old,
heading home
from school, from church,
from Helen Reis's house, who knows,
but I'm definitely walking along a sandy path,
thinking: I'm going to be an artist.
I have one dress, one pair of shoes,
and one vision that I don't recognize as poetic:
a papaya tree ripe with fruit beneath bright sun and sparrows.
It would be mine forever, because it was good-without-end,
like rosebed, a fishhook word,
conveying heat, noontime, fangs—
an affliction, but only in tiny droplets
because the Virgin was crushing the Devil
under her rosy heel.
All I did was bring my father his tinder and tobacco
and he said: "Wow! A girl worth her weight in gold!"
He could be unfair sometimes, but he'd also spend the whole
    afternoon
hunting for *sabugueiro* to cure my cough.
It looks like I'm about to get sad,
too listless even to wash greens,
tempted toward a stricter abstinence:
won't eat, won't talk, won't laugh—
even if the Pope dresses up like Carmen Miranda.
Virgin Mary! I'm nothing but time-fodder,
time is going to eat me up!
Help me birth this litter of voices, please
—if not, this connivance of shadows will kidnap me,
seize my old outlook and ready passion.

Mater Dolorosa

This taffy
tastes like coconut, Mama.
Did you put coconut in it?
—Coconut nothing.
—Did you have a big party when you got married?
—Sure. Huge.
—What was it like?
—Nothing. We just got married.
—That's all?
—Yup, that's it.
One time we went on a picnic.
She made meatballs
for us to put on bread.
I remember the curve of the river
and sitting on the sand.
It was Sunday,
she wasn't exhausted,
she patiently answered all my questions.
If heaven is simply that,
it will be perfect.

Chamberpot

At midnight, José dos Reis
—my secret boyfriend—
comes to serenade me.
Papa coughs
and rattles the chamberpot.
Lord, how embarrassing—
his little waterfall,
collards in the garden
icy with dew and fear.
I make like a dead saint.
My heaven is gothic
and on fire.

Invitational

Looking out through the rain I see
the steeple of Bom Jesus,
a few trees, houses,
and a desolation sweeps over me.
A whole life to arrive here
on this Sunday,
in this city without history
in this rain,
a harbinger of fear
but not lightning,
since it's the gentle kind.
Is death unappealable?
Can there be there no alibi, no turn of events,
no unexpected bearer of good news?
Four boys duck into the bushes
and emerge smoking,
brushing stuff off their clothes.
A black woman climbs a ladder, an old man, too,
someone tosses trash
through a hole in the wall,
everything just as it was in nineteen hundred and seventy-six.
Why do we make mistakes?
I wanted to write seventeen hundred and ninety-six—
what threw me off the track?
There's a smell in the air
which—to my surprise—no one else seems to notice,
metallic, a smell of iron that burns my nostrils.
Nothing makes any sense,
I want a big basin
to gather all the pieces and assemble them

once the visitors go home.
No one's playing tricks, because there's no one here,
it's an old silent film,
the lips move but that's it.
Hear me, Lord Jesus. Do I exist?
I haven't dreamed in a long time—do I exist?
Answer me, take pity on me,
give me back my old joy, my comfortable fears,
not this, please no, I'm too weak.
Hear me, poor little me,
Our Lady of the Conception, come to my aid.

Christ's Passion

In spite of the bowl
so white,
its porcelain
so fine,
there they sit at the bottom
exuding majesty,
existing only in the plural:
feces.
If I muster even a grain
of happiness,
they pounce on me right away:
"Lower your voice,
  you're not as powerful as you think."
My martyrdom is bloodless
but pains just the same.

Application for Adoption

Oh, how I long for the days
when I had a mother,
wrinkled skin,
hair tied back,
knuckles like knots,
so old
she could almost be the mother of God
—if she weren't such a sinner.
But this old woman is me,
my mother died young,
her eyes still bright,
face filled with fear.
Lord! I thought
children were the only ones called
orphans.

Woman at Nightfall

Dear God,
don't punish me for saying
my life was so lovely!
We're human,
our verbs have tenses,
they're not like Yours,
eternal.

Meditation of the King Among His Troops

The great deeds of memorable men
can be chalked up to their biographers.
Biographies are made of wishes,
even those of assassins and saints.
Life—pure, raw,
naked life—
is only gravel,
a shadow play
set in motion by the hands of a child.
Just as birds migrate to warmer climes
under invisible commands, we carry on,
and even standing in line we're happy.

Rebuke of Pride

Whatever reveals itself immediately,
pulsating, finished,
cacophonies leaking preciousness,
sneers at the poet
busy wiping his texticles:
Oh, buffoon,
in poetry as in painting
the eyes belong on the belly.
Let it fly!

October

"El monito," I would say
 if I spoke Spanish
 but all I know is Portuguese
 and how to beat one coconut
 against another, ignorant
 and daring.
 October brings me desires,
 secret and confessable.
 I shriek loudly
 for the same reasons as the cicadas.

Human Rights

I know God lives in me
as in no other house.
I am His countryside,
His alchemical vessel,
and, to His joy,
His two eyes.
But this handwriting is mine.

Just Like a Man

I ate in front of the TV
without using a knife,
plate after plateful,
like truck drivers who talk with their mouths full,
and I watched the show till the end.
Into the wee hours
I watched loutish emcees
say to swivel-hipped girls
"Here, sweetheart, hold my microphone."
Afterward, I fell asleep and dreamed
I was flying, pursued by soldiers,
terrified I'd get tangled in electric wires.
I woke feeling queasy and eclipsed.
A real man
would have dreamed of those swiveling hips.

Ex-Voto

One hot, bright, Sunday afternoon
I was ambushed
by pressing intestines, throes of nausea and weeping,
the desire to tear my hair and strip naked
in the middle of my life and howl
until bone dry:
What do you want from me, God?
Once I stopped crying,
the man who sat waiting said,
"You're so sensitive, that's why you get short of breath."
Which started me crying again, because it was true
and also a lie,
and therefore only half consoling.
Breathe deeply, he urged, splash some cold water on your face,
let's take a walk around the block, it's psychological.
What ex-voto can I bring to the Cathedral
if I'm not sick but still need a cure?
My devout friend has turned Buddhist,
I'm rooting for her to get disillusioned
and go back to praying Catholic prayers with me.
I could never be a Buddhist,
for fear of not suffering, for fear of getting all Zen.
Is there really such a thing as a happy saint or is it just the
     biographers
who paint them as such sunny saps?
The state of Minas Gerais is full of terrible things,
Mercy Mountain afflicts me.
Boulders and boulders
of such immediate beauty,
and then buildings sprung straight from hell,

courtesy of the uncreator of the world.
And there's that little boy who can't hang on much longer,
he's going to die, too weak to suck
the string of dark flesh that's supposed to be a breast,
lost to flies.
My heart is good
but can't believe it.
My man showers me with gifts,
why am I given so much
when what I deserve is solitary confinement?
Words? No, I said—I can only accept weeping.
So why ever did I wipe my eyes
at the sight of the climbing rosebush
and that other thing I didn't want—
no way did I want it right then,
the poem,
my ex-voto,
not the shape of what's sick
but of what's sound in me
which I push and push away,
pressed by the same force
that works against the beauty of the boulders.
Both God and the world are begging for love,
which is why I'm richer than either one.
I alone can say to the stone:
you are beautiful to affliction.
just as I can say to Him:
You are beautiful, beautiful, so beautiful!
I almost understand why I'm gasping for air.
Choosing the words to describe my agony,
I'm breathing easier already.
Some of us God wants sick; others he wants writing.

Anamnesis

At the calmest hour of the day
the startled chicken
veered madly
across the yard.
It was a barred rock,
my mother was still alive,
I was very small.
At a loss to explain such nonsense,
she said:
"Nitwit chicken."
I burst into tears,
it was like having no undies.

Holy Icon

Despite my desire
for repentance and joy,
I woke up belligerent,
wild to find a big knife.
The dog could tell,
the boy, too,
running for cover on his mother's lap.
God, did I just ask You
why You're not listening?
Or was it someone else praying for me?
Watching from her frame on the wall,
the Madonna offered her boy
to my blade.
I, who raved nightly
in the pluperfect
on account of Portugal having signed
The Treaty of Tordesillas,
burst out laughing at the squash
—as much the word as the thing—
and suddenly I simmered down, no longer concerned
that it's not called dumpster instead.
Like a lunatic who's all at once
done with orderlies and pills,
I sat cutting cane with my big knife,
content to suck sweetness in the shade.

Saint Christopher Transit

I don't want to die ever,
for fear of losing the riches
unwinding outside this window.
Was that the Pony Bar, Bony Bar, or Tony Bar?
Across from the train station
the feed store announces where it's from:
Woodland.
Reading essence in a name
we get half-truths,
because the bus stops
and life doesn't,
because life is You, unnamable!
My husband really likes sex,
but he's also capable
of prolonged abstinence.
That guy tending his garden
with a hatred so profound
that he almost looks innocent
means to guillotine the neighbor woman
with the radiant window.
Does any of this move You?
An hour and a half on the road
and life is so good it hurts.
The fields are parched
but invincible
in their power to take me back . . .
To You? To childhood?
To the Fatherland, to the Kingdom of Heaven.
What can I do? This is a poem.
I'm really hungry, I'd like to attend Mass right here and now.

A couple of workers give me the thumbs-up,
everything grows even more peaceful.
Did I fall asleep?
Nodding off is so unsightly.
That scientist really made me happy when he said
"Beauty is energy."
I knew this without knowing,
and it's going to be serious help.
The bus stops again,
bulldozers scrape
the earth ever more pure.
Sure, they're knocking down trees,
but ecology can wait.
The power of those machines!
The way they heave the trees,
everyone stock still, watching.
It's good to see a man at heavy labor,
a woman looking after her child—
instruction left to the priest.
I'm the same as when young,
so ignorant and so smart.
If the bus is running late,
so what, I don't care,
I went, I came back, but most of all
I want to stay right here.

Spiritual Exercise

Mary,
Pray your Son to show me God the Father.
Images arrive:
a man, a vignette, a musical instrument,
what seems a feather fan
turns out to be a cobra head.
I want to see the Father, I insist.
Pray your Son to show me the Father.
A tooth, a vulva,
a bunch of turnips appear,
born as I was from nothing.
Mary, where do turnips come from?
Where is the Father?
Where did I come from?
A horse of sun moves on the wall.
Is it the Father?
No,
it's just a shadow, already disappearing.
Is the Father a factory, then?
My father used to say: O Father!
And raise his arms reverently.
Grandpa, too: God our Father!
And he'd take of his hat.
So one father leads back to another
and another, and yet another,
and then, millions of fathers later, at last to Adam,
who is me, waking from a dream,
just when "dawn shone through, blood-red and cool,"
daughter of a Parnassian,
which so enchanted me when I was a girl,

daughter of a railroad man,
as exhausted now
as a green-grocer at noontime:
ai, father,
help me hawk the rest
of these squash,
drum the idea of seeing Father-God
out of my head,
give me a smoke and some coffee.

The State of May

Salvation operates in the abyss.
In this indescribable place,
night's power of evil compelled me
to long for and loathe the world.
The grass was vibrating
but not for me,
nor for the afternoon songbirds.
Dogs, children, yowls
were disowning me.
And so I prayed: Preserve me, Mother of God,
from the tempter and his tricks.
Lady, are you lost?
asked the boy.
The path's over here.
I came back to myself
and recognized the stones of morning.

Neopelican

One day,
just as I'd seen a ship once,
unforgettable,
I saw a lion, close up.
He was reclining,
a raw individual soul.
A strong smell, not sweet,
mix of blood and vinegar.
I was exultant, because I had no words
and not having them would prolong my delight:
a lion!
Only a god is like this, I thought.
I superimposed over the lion
a whole new animal
radiating the aura
of his ripe color.
Have mercy on me, I prayed to him,
constricted, grateful
to be small once more.
This super-human faith lasted a minute.
I speak with a throb:
I saw no lion,
I saw the Lord!

Acknowledgments

Some of these translations have been previously published, often in earlier versions, in the following journals or books:

5 AM: "The Meticulous One" and *"Syllabication"*

American Poetry Review: "Furious with Jonathan," "The Mystical Rose," "The Sacrifice," "Saint Christopher Transit," and "Two o'Clock in the Afternoon in Brazil"

Bomb: "Meditation Verging on a Poem" (as "Meditation Beside a Poem"), "Nap with Flowers," and "Opus Dei"

The Cortland Review (online, in text and audio): "Sleeping Beauty"

The Ecco Anthology of International Poetry (Ecco Press, 2010): "The Tenacious Devil Who Doesn't Exist"

Harvard Review (online): "Heraldry"

Image: "Buried Treasure," "Divine Wrath" and "Domus"

The Literary Olympians: An International Anthology (Fox-Brown & Company, 1992): "The Transfer of the Body"

The Massachusetts Review: "The Birth of the Poem"

Metamorphoses: "The Battle," "God Does Not Reject the Work of His Hands," and "Responsory"

Mead (online): "Chamberpot," "The Dark of Night," and "Portunhol"

Water-Stone Review: "God's Assistant" and "Mural"

Other books from Tupelo Press

Fasting for Ramadan: Notes from a Spiritual Practice, Kazim Ali
Circle's Apprentice, Dan Beachy-Quick
The Vital System, CM Burroughs
Severance Songs, Joshua Corey
Atlas Hour, Carol Ann Davis
Sanderlings, Geri Doran
The Flight Cage, Rebecca Dunham
The Posthumous Affair (novel), James Friel
The Us, Joan Houlihan
Nothing Can Make Me Do This (novel), David Huddle
Meridian, Kathleen Jesme
Dancing in Odessa, Ilya Kaminsky
A God in the House: Poets Talk About Faith,
     edited by Ilya Kaminsky and Katherine Towler
Manoleria, Daniel Khalastchi
domina Un/blued, Ruth Ellen Kocher
Phyla of Joy, Karen An-hwei Lee
Body Thesaurus, Jennifer Militello
After Urgency, Rusty Morrison
Lucky Fish, Aimee Nezhukumatathil
Long Division, Alan Michael Parker
Intimate: An American Family Photo Album, Paisley Rekdal
Thrill-Bent (novel), Jan Richman
Calendars of Fire, Lee Sharkey
Cream of Kohlrabi: Stories, Floyd Skloot
Babel's Moon, Brandon Som
Swallowing the Sea (essays), Lee Upton
Butch Geography, Stacey Waite
Archicembalo, G. C. Waldrep
Dogged Hearts, Ellen Doré Watson

See our complete backlist at www.tupelopress.org

ADÉLIA DORÉ JENKINS

ADÉLIA PRADO has authored eight volumes of poetry and seven volumes of literary prose in Portuguese. The first in her family of laborers to see the ocean or go to college, Prado has lived all her life in the provincial industrial city of Divinópolis in Minas Gerais, Brazil. She has degrees in Philosophy and Religious Education from the University of Divinópolis, and she worked for many years as a schoolteacher. In 2013, the Griffin Trust for Excellence in Poetry is honoring Prado with a Lifetime Achievement Award, previously given to Seamus Heaney, Adrienne Rich, and Tomas Tranströmer, among others.

ELLEN DORÉ WATSON was hailed by *Library Journal* as one of "24 Poets for the 21st Century." Her collections of poetry include *Ladder Music* and *We Live in Bodies* (Alice James, 2001 and 2002), *This Sharpening* (Tupelo, 2006), and most recently *Dogged Hearts* (book and audio book: Tupelo, 2010). She has also translated a dozen books, including *The Alphabet in the Park: Selected Poems of Adélia Prado* (Wesleyan University Press, 1990) and works by Brazilian poet Ignácio de Loyola Brandão as well as contemporary Arabic poetry (co-translated with Saadi Simawe). She is the Poetry and Translation Editor for *The Massachusetts Review* and the director of The Poetry Center at Smith College in Northampton, Massachusetts.